TOPPERS 2

by Lynda Milligan & Nancy Smith

Credits

Sharon Holmes – Editor, Technical Illustrator
Lexie Foster – Cover Design, Illustration, Photo Stylist, Quilt Design
Susie Johnson – Photo Stylist, Quilt Design
Christine Scott – Editorial Assistant
Sandi Fruehling – Copy Reader
Brad Bartholomew – Photographer

Thanks

Sewing & Machine Quilting – Ann Petersen, Jane Dumler, Katie Wells,
Susan Auskaps, Sue Williams, Courtenay Hughes, Karol Ann Frederichs
Long-arm Machine Quilting – Sandi Fruehling, Carolyn Schmitt, Susan F. Geddes, Kay Morrison

SPECIAL THANKS – We would like to extend our gratitude to everyone at
Crate and Barrel in Littleton, Colorado. For some time now, they have graciously
allowed us to photograph our quilts in their beautiful store. Thank you!

POSSIBILITIES ®

…Fabric designers for AvLyn, Inc., publishers of DreamSpinners®
patterns & I'll Teach Myself™ & Possibilities® books…

Home of Great American Quilt Factory, Inc.

Toppers 2

Published in the United States of America by Possibilities®, Denver, Colorado
Library of Congress Control Number: 2003102935
ISBN: 1-880972-51-4

Dedication

We would like to dedicate this book to a very special employee, Aina Martin. Aina is Lynda's mom, and her job is Accounts Payable and Payroll. On Accounts Payable days, her job is somewhat thankless as she writes check after check, but, come payday, she is everyone's friend. Thank you very much, Mom, for the support you give us and the expertise and accuracy with which you do your job. We don't know what we would do without you. By the way, the bank statement is here!

How to Use Toppers 2

Thank you for the overwhelming success of our book, *Toppers*.

You keep asking for more Toppers, so here they are.

Toppers started out as small quilts that are fast to make and can be combined with simple bed covers. They evolved into versatile quilts used many ways—draped over the back of a sofa or overstuffed chair, placed over the pillows on a bed as a special sham, and even used on tables as ornamental or utilitarian covers. They are fun to make, and many of them are quick and easy. You can change your decor with your mood or with the season.

Pillow Toppers cover the pillows and also look very nice folded at the foot of the bed. When using a Pillow Topper on a couch, the plain upper part falls over the back of the couch to help keep it in place. If you want to make a Pillow Topper into a wall hanging, simply leave off the plain part. We have included directions for simple squares and half-square triangle quilts on page 3.

These are wonderful, quick-to-make bed covers to use with any of the Pillow Toppers in the book, and a smaller version can be made for a throw to coordinate with a Pillow Topper displayed on a couch. The square Toppers look nice over purchased coverlets, and they also make great wall hangings.

We want to encourage you to design your own Toppers. Feel free to substitute a different block in the patchwork Toppers. Find a block or design a block that is the same size as the one you are replacing. You could also substitute an applique block of your choice. Instead of placing the blocks side by side, piece them into a square Topper. Have fun changing colors on any of the Toppers. Sherbet Stars could be made patriotic by using red, white, and blue fabrics. Enjoy exercising your creativity with these Toppers, and be sure to send us photos of how you are using them.

We are sure you will have many more ideas for using our patterns! Happy stitching!

Big Squares Quilts

Photos on pages 26 and 32. Make one of these easy quilts based on 8″ squares to go with any of the pillow toppers that appear later in the book. They are "comforter" size—that is, they cover the mattress only, and they go under the pillows.

Use fabric with 42″ usable width. When strips appear in cutting list, cut crossgrain strips (selvage to selvage).

	T	D/Q	K
Size	72x88″	96x96″	104x96″
8″ squares	99	144	156
Yardage			
Squares - 11 fabrics	⅞ yd ea	1⅛ yd ea	1⅛ yd ea
Backing	5⅝ yd	8⅞ yd	8⅞ yd
Binding	¾ yd	⅞ yd	⅞ yd
Batting	78x94″	102x102″	110x102″
Cutting			
Squares - 8½″	99	144	156
Binding - 2½″ strips	9	10	11

Directions

Use ¼″ seam allowance.

1. ASSEMBLE:

   a. Stitch squares into

   Twin - 11 horizontal rows of 9
   D/Q - 12 horizontal rows of 12
   King - 12 horizontal rows of 13

   b. Press seam allowances of odd rows to left and seam allowances of even rows to right.

   c. Stitch rows together. Press.

2. FINISH: Piece backing vertically to same size as batting. Use your favorite layering and quilting methods. Bind with ⅜″ seam allowance.

Big Triangles Quilts

Photo on page 10. Make one of these easy quilts based on 8″ squares to go with any of the pillow toppers that appear later in the book. They are "comforter" size—that is, they cover the mattress only, and they go under the pillows.

Use fabric with 42″ usable width. When strips appear in cutting list, cut crossgrain strips (selvage to selvage).

	T	D/Q	K
Size	72x88″	96x96″	104x96″
8″ units	99	144	156
Yardage			
Squares - 11 fabrics	⅞ yd ea	1⅛ yd ea	1⅛ yd ea
Backing	5⅝ yd	8⅞ yd	8⅞ yd
Binding	¾ yd	⅞ yd	⅞ yd
Batting	78x94″	102x102″	110x102″
Cutting *Cut in HALF diagonally			
Squares - *8⅞″	99	144	156
Binding - 2½″ strips	9	10	11

Directions

Use ¼″ seam allowance.

1. SQUARES: For all quilts, stitch triangles into squares using fabrics as desired. Press.

2. ASSEMBLE:

   a. Stitch squares into

   Twin - 11 horizontal rows of 9
   D/Q - 12 horizontal rows of 12
   King - 12 horizontal rows of 13

   b. Press seam allowances of odd rows to left and seam allowances of even rows to right.

   c. Stitch rows together. Press.

3. FINISH: Piece backing vertically to same size as batting. Use your favorite layering and quilting methods. Bind with ⅜″ seam allowance.

Star Dance
TOPPER

Photo on page 4.

Use fabric with 42″ usable width. When strips appear in cutting list, cut crossgrain strips (selvage to selvage).

Note: To provide flexibility in color use, enough yardage has been figured for cutting an extra strip of each fabric. There will be leftover fabric.

	T	D/Q/K
Size	48 x 48″	60 x 60″
6″ blocks	64	100

Yardage

Bright pastels		
Stars		
Yellow, peach, pink, & pink-purples		
12 fabrics	⅓ yd each	½ yd each
Background		
Blue, green, teal, & blue-purples		
15 fabrics	⅓ yd each	½ yd each
Backing	3¼ yd	4 yd
Binding	⅝ yd	⅝ yd
Batting	54 x 54″	66 x 66″

Cutting Paper piecing pattern on page 56

Stars - from each fabric		
2½″ strips	3	5
Background - from each fabric		
5½″ strips	1	1
2½″ strips	1	2
Binding - 2½″ strips	6	7

Directions

Use ¼″ seam allowance.

1. PLANNING: Use coloring diagram on page 6 to plan color placement. Each star is made of 1 fabric and is formed at the corners of 4 blocks, making each block dependent on its neighbor. The background of each block is comprised of 2 colors, a trapezoid and a triangle of each color. Make accurate copies of paper piecing pattern on page 56 [T 128 copies] [D/Q/K 200 copies].

2. SUBCUTTING: Cut 5½″ squares from 5½″ strips [T 64 squares] [D/Q/K 100 squares]. Cut squares in half diagonally. Save the remaining strips and/or parts of strips for cutting additional 2½″ strips as needed for trapezoids.

3. BLOCKS: Paper piece half-blocks. Use the background fabric triangles for the corner triangles, the background fabric strips for the trapezoids, and the star fabric strips for the diamonds. Stitch half-blocks into blocks. Press.

4. ROWS: Stitch blocks into rows [T 8 rows of 8] [D/Q/K 10 rows of 10]. Stitch rows together. Press.

5. FINISH: Piece backing to same size as batting. Use your favorite layering and quilting methods. Bind with ⅜″ seam allowance.

TWIN SIZE

D/Q/K SIZE

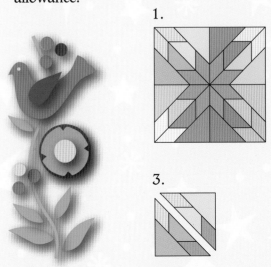

1.

3.

See page 7 for quilted pillowcase directions.

5

Star Dance
COLORING DIAGRAM

TWIN SIZE   D/Q/K SIZE

Folk Art Fantasy
QUILTED PILLOWCASE

Photos on pages 4 & 20.
Standard Size: 20x30″
Use fabric with 42½″ usable width.

Yardage for 1 pillowcase

Main fabric, binding	¾ yd
Applique background	⅓ yd
Appliques as desired	⅛-¼ yd each
Stems	⅛ yd
Lining	1½ yd
Batting	33 x 46″

Cutting Patterns on pages 42-44

Main fabric	21½ x 42½″
Binding	2½ x 42½″
Applique background	9½ x 42½″
Appliques	as desired

Directions

Use ¼″ seam allowance unless otherwise noted.

1. APPLIQUE: Fold applique background in half lengthwise and mark center. Using Folk Art Fantasy designs as desired, applique. If a stem is desired, cut a piece ⅜-½″ wide from a fused piece of stem fabric. Gently shape the curves before fusing to applique background.

2. ASSEMBLE: Determine desired direction of finished pillowcases for bird applique. Stitch applique background to main fabric (42½″ sides). Press.

3. FINISH: Cut lining to same size as batting. Layer and quilt as desired. Trim backing and batting to same size as top. Fold pillowcase in half lengthwise, right sides together. Leaving end with applique open, stitch side and end using ⅜″ seam allowance. Turn right side out. Bind edge using ⅜″ seam allowance.

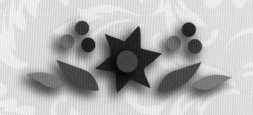

1.

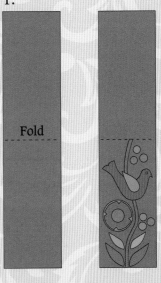

Fold

2.

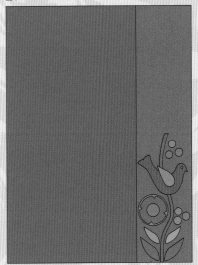

3.

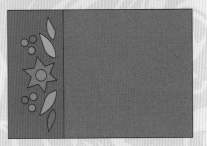

7

BLUE DAHLIA
TOPPER

Photo on page 8.

Use fabric with 42″ usable width. When strips appear in cutting list, cut crossgrain strips (selvage to selvage).

Patterns are given for fusible web applique, reversed and ready to be traced. Be sure to have plenty of fusible web on hand if using this method. Reverse patterns and add seam allowance if doing hand applique.

		T/D	Q/K
Size		61x73″	73x86″
9″ applique blocks		12	20
9″ star blocks		20	30
Side setting triangles		14	18
Corner setting triangles		4	4

Yardage

Blues	flower petals - 2 fabrics	⅓ yd each	½ yd each
	applique background	1 yd	1⅝ yd
	star blocks - 5 fabrics	⅜ yd each	⅜ yd each
	Border 2	1⅛ yd	1¼ yd
Rusts	blocks - 5 fabrics	½ yd each	⅝ yd each
Peach	blocks	½ yd	⅝ yd
Gold #1	flower centers, Border 1	⅝ yd	⅞ yd
Gold #2	blocks	1 yd	1⅓ yd
Backing		4⅝ yd	5½ yd
Binding		⅝ yd	¾ yd
Batting		67x79″	79x92″

Cutting Pattern on page 50

Blues		
Flower petals - total from 2 fabrics	108	180
	36 reversed	60 reversed
Applique background - 9½″ squares	12	20
Star blocks, side & corner setting triangles		
**4¼″ squares from each fabric	12	16
Border 2 - 4½″ strips	7	8
Rusts		
Blocks - 3½″ squares from each fabric	16	24
Setting triangles - 3½″ sqs from each fabric	3	4
*3⅞″ sqs from each fabric	4	5
Small flower centers	12	20
Peach - blocks - 3½″ squares	20	30
side setting triangles - *3⅞″ squares	7	9
corner setting triangles - *3″ squares	2	2
Gold #1		
Large flower centers, "dots"	12 sets	20 sets
Border 1 - 1½″ strips	6	8
Gold #2 - Blocks, side & corner		
setting triangles - **4¼″ squares	56	80
Binding - 2½″ strips	7	9

*Cut in HALF diagonally **Cut in QUARTERS diagonally

Directions

Use ¼″ seam allowance.

1. APPLIQUE BLOCKS: Use 12 petals per flower, 9 and 3 reversed.

2. STAR BLOCKS: See diagram. Press.

3. SIDE SETTING TRIANGLES: See diagram. Press.

4. CORNER SETTING TRIANGLES: See diagram. Press.

5. ROWS: Lay blocks and setting triangles on floor. Applique blocks should be set [T/D 4 rows of 3] [Q/K 5 rows of 4]. Stitch into diagonal rows. Stitch rows together. Press.

6. BORDER 1: Stitch border strips to same length as Topper. Make 2. Stitch to sides of Topper. Repeat at top and bottom. Press.

7. BORDER 2: Repeat Step 6.

8. FINISH: Piece backing vertically to same size as batting. Use your favorite layering and quilting methods. Bind with ⅜″ seam allowance.

T/D SIZE

Diagrams continued on page 25

Apartment Life
PILLOW TOPPER

Photo on page 10.

Use fabric with 42″ usable width. When strips appear in cutting list, cut crossgrain strips (selvage to selvage) unless otherwise noted.

Patterns are given for fusible web applique, reversed and ready to be traced. Be sure to have plenty of fusible web on hand if using this method. Reverse patterns and add seam allowance if doing hand applique.

		T	D/Q	K
Size		48x40″	70x40″	88x40″
Yardage				
Blue		1⅜ yd	2 yd	2½ yd
Light brown		1⅜ yd	2⅛ yd	2⅝ yd
Dark brown		½ yd	⅝ yd	⅝ yd
Green #1	house	⅓ yd	⅓ yd	⅓ yd
Green #2	grass	⅙ yd	⅙ yd	¼ yd
Greens #3 & up	2-3 fabrics	⅙ yd ea	⅙ yd ea	⅙ yd ea
Rust #1	house	⅓ yd	⅓ yd	⅓ yd
Rusts #2 & up	3-4 fabrics	⅙ yd ea	⅙ yd ea	⅙ yd ea
Brown #1	house	⅓ yd	⅓ yd	⅓ yd
Browns & tans	3-4 fabrics	⅙ yd ea	⅙ yd ea	⅙ yd ea
Med & lt blue		⅛ yd ea	⅛ yd ea	⅛ yd ea
Backing		1⅝ yd	2¼ yd	2¾ yd
Binding		½ yd	⅝ yd	⅝ yd
Batting		52x44″	74x44″	92x44″

Cutting Patterns on pages 54-56

		T	D/Q	K
Blue	background	17x40½″	17x62½″	17x80½″
Light brown	background	16½x44½″	16½x66½″	16½x84½″
	2½″ strips cut on lengthwise grain	2	2	2
Dark brown	border - 2½″ strips	5	6	7
Green #1	house	1	1	1-2
Green #2	2″ strips	1-2	2	2-3
Rust #1	house	1	1	1-2
Brown #1	house	1	1	1-2
Others	appliques as desired			
Binding	2½″ strips	5	6	7

Directions

Use ¼″ seam allowance.

1. **APPLIQUE:** Arrange pieces as shown in diagram for queen size, placing bottom edges of houses and tree trunks even with bottom raw edge of blue background piece. For twin, place 3 houses, then place 2 trees between them. For king, place 5 houses, then place 4 trees between them.

2. **GRASS & BROWN BACKGROUND:** Stitch grass strips together end to end. Trim to [T 40½″] [D/Q 62½″] [K 80½″]. Stitch to bottom edge of blue background. Trim 1 light brown background strip to same length as grass. Stitch to bottom edge of grass. Cut light brown strips to fit sides of house panel. Stitch to sides of panel. Press. Stitch light brown background to top. Press.

3. **BORDER:** Cut border strips to fit sides of Topper. Make 2. Stitch to sides of Topper. Stitch border strips together to fit top and bottom. Stitch to Topper. Press.

4. **FINISH:** Cut backing to same size as batting. Use your favorite layering and quilting methods. Bind with ⅜″ seam allowance.

Quilt

Use directions on page 3 for Big Triangles Quilt. To add a border and maintain the chart sizes, make the quilt one row narrower and one row shorter, then add a 4″ border.

D/Q SIZE

11

Sherbet Stars
TOPPER

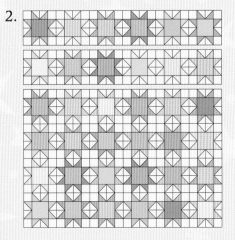

Photo on page 12.

Use fabric with 42″ usable width. When strips appear in cutting list, cut crossgrain strips (selvage to selvage).

		T	D/Q/K
Size		47 x 47″	53 x 53″
6″ blocks		25	36

Yardage
		T	D/Q/K
Cream		2¼ yd	2⅝ yd
Pastels - 12 or more fabrics		¼ yd each	¼ yd each
Backing		3⅛ yd	3½ yd
Batting		51x51″	57x57″

Cutting
		T	D/Q/K
Cream			
Blocks	2″ squares	116	160
	*2⅜″ squares	116	160
Border 1	2½″ strips	4	4
Border 3	6½″ strips	4	4-5
Pastels			
Border 2	1¼″ strips	6 total	7 total
Binding	2¼″ strips	7 total	8 total
Blocks	*2⅜″ squares	29 sets of 4	40 sets of 4
	3½″ squares	29 total	40 total

*Cut in HALF diagonally

ee page 41 for quilted
llowcase directions.

Directions

Use ¼″ seam allowance.

1. **BLOCKS:** Make [T 29] [D/Q/K 40] blocks following diagram. Press.

2. **ROWS:** Stitch blocks into rows [T 5 rows of 5] [D/Q/K 6 rows of 6]. Stitch rows together. Press.

3. **BORDER 1:** Cut 2 Border 1 strips to same length as Topper. Stitch to sides of Topper. Repeat at top and bottom. Press.

4. **BORDER 2:** Cut pastel strips into pieces 2½″ to 4½″ long. Stitch pieces together to same length as Topper. Make 2. Stitch to sides of Topper. Repeat at top and bottom. Press.

5. **BORDER 3:** Cut 4 Border 3 strips to same length/width as Topper. Stitch to sides of Topper. Stitch star blocks ends of remaining borders and stitch borders to top and bottom. Press.

6. **FINISH:** Piece backing to same size as batting. Layer and quilt as desired. Sub-cut binding strips into pieces 2½-4½″ long. Stitch binding pieces end to end in random order. Press seam allowances open. Press in half lengthwise, wrong sides together and bind quilt using ¼″ seam allowance.

1. For each block:

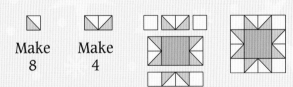

Make 8   Make 4

2.

D/Q/K SIZE

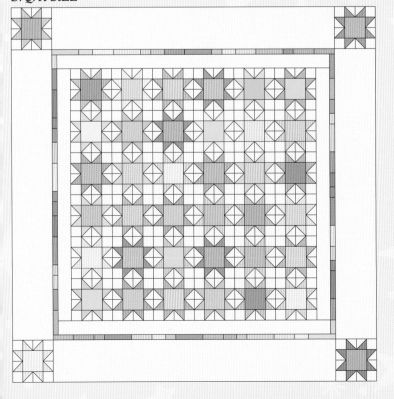

13

Black & Tan
PILLOW TOPPER

Photo on page 14.

Use fabric with 42″ usable width. When strips appear in cutting list, cut crossgrain strips (selvage to selvage) unless otherwise noted.

Note: Use your favorite half-square triangle method for accurate 1″ and 2″ units. Cutting chart gives sizes to cut when stitching 2 triangles together; ignore these entries if using another method and increase yardage if needed.

		T	D/Q	K
Size		48x40″	70x40″	88x40″
10″ blocks		3	5	6
Yardage				
Black #1		1⅞ yd	2½ yd	3 yd
Black #2		½ yd	½ yd	⅝ yd
Gold		⅔ yd	⅞ yd	1⅛ yd
Brown		⅔ yd	⅞ yd	⅞ yd
Lt rust		⅛ yd	⅛ yd	⅛ yd
Print		¼ yd	¼ yd	¼ yd
Cream		⅓ yd	⅜ yd	½ yd
Backing		1⅝ yd	2¼ yd	2¾ yd
Binding		½ yd	⅝ yd	⅝ yd
Batting		52x44″	74x44″	92x44″
Cutting	*Cut in HALF diagonally			
Black #1	upper background	48½x17½″	70½x17½″	88½x17½″
	setting triangles			
	3½″ squares	4	8	10
	3½x8″	8	16	20
	*8″ squares	2	2	2
	border units			
	3x42″ cut on lengthwise grain	3	4	5
	coping strips in sizes needed			
Black #2	star points			
	*2⅞″ squares	12	20	24
	strip sets			
	4″ strips	2	2	2
Gold	star blocks, setting triangles			
	*2⅞″ squares	14	24	29
	2½″ squares	12	20	24
	border units			
	4″ strips	3	4	5
Brown	star blocks, setting triangles			
	1½″ squares	24	40	48
	*1⅞″ squares	36	64	78
	2½″ squares	6	10	12
	strip sets			
	2½″ strips	4	4	4
Lt rust	star blocks			
	2½″ squares	6	10	12
Print	star blocks			
	1½x4½″	12	20	24
Cream	star blocks, setting triangles			
	1½″ squares	16	28	34
	*1⅞″ squares	32	56	68
Binding	2½″ strips	5	6	7

Directions

Use ¼″ seam allowance.

Diagrams on pages 16-17.

1. BLOCKS: Make [T 3] [D/Q 5] [K 6] blocks as shown. Press.

2. SETTING TRIANGLES: Make [T 4] [D/Q 8] [K 10] setting triangles as shown. Press. Do not trim ends of rectangles.

3. ASSEMBLE: Stitch blocks, setting triangles, and corner triangles into diagonal rows as shown. Press. Trim extending ends of rectangles. Treat this bias edge with care. Measure width of block row. Add coping strips, if necessary, to ends of row to make it the same width as upper background piece [T 48½″] [D/Q 70½″] [K 88½″].

4. BORDER UNITS

   a. Make 2 strip sets as shown using 4″ black #2 strips and 2½″ brown strips. Press seam allowances toward brown strips.

   b. Crosscut strip sets into 2½″ segments.

   c. Stitch [T 18] [D/Q 26] [K 32] segments together, matching raw edge of each segment to raw edge of seam allowance of previous segment as shown. Press seam allowances open. Save or make extra segments for lengthening border units if necessary.

Directions continued on page 17.

1. For each block:

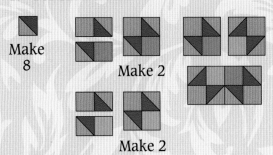

Make 8

Make 2

Make 2

Make 2

Diagrams continued on page 16.

1. For each block, continued:

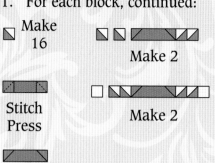

Make 16

Make 2

Stitch
Press

Make 2

Make 4

Make: [T 3]
[D/Q 5] [K 6]

2. For each setting triangle:

Make 4   Make 1   Make 1

Make: [T 4]
[D/Q 8] [K 10]

3.

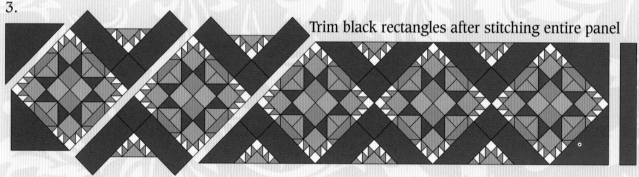

Trim black rectangles after stitching entire panel

Add copin strip at eac end if neede

4a-b.

Make 2
Strip Sets

2½″

4c. Match raw edges

Press seam allowances open

4d-e.   Measure

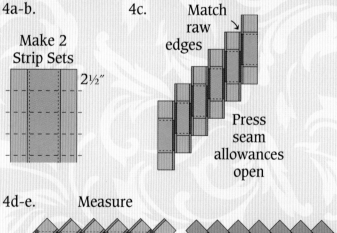

Mark center line, then cut on line

4f.

Trim symetrically to same length as upper background and block row

4g.

Strip set seam allowances not shown

Stitch black strip to brown side from point to point, patchwork piece on top.

Trim to ¼″seam allowance.

Trim black strip to 1¼″ from SEAM.

Stitch gold strip to black side from point to point, patchwork piece on top.

Trim to ¼″seam allowance.

Trim gold strip to 2¼″ from SEAM.

TWIN SIZE

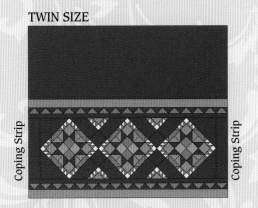

Coping Strip   Coping Strip

DOUBLE/QUEEN SIZE

Possible Coping Strip   Possible Coping Strip

KING SIZE

Coping Strip   Coping Strip

d. Measure length of unit between points as shown in diagram. If less than width of upper background and block row, add enough segments to border unit to make it longer than [T 48½″] [D/Q 70½″] [K 88½″]. It will be trimmed to fit later.

e. Mark center of unit on wrong side. Cut on mark. See diagram.

f. Trim length of border units symmetrically to same length as block row and top background [T 48½″] [D/Q 70½″] [K 88½″].

g. Stitch 3″ black #1 strips end to end. Repeat with 4″ gold strips. Cut 2 of each color to same length as pieced border units.

Pin black strip to brown triangle side of each strip of patchwork, right sides together. Stitch from point to point. See diagram. Trim to ¼″ seam allowance. Press seam allowance toward black strip. Trim black strip to 1¼″ from SEAM.

With right sides together and raw edges even, stitch gold strip to black triangle side of patchwork strip. Trim seam allowance to ¼″. Press seam allowance toward gold strip. Trim gold strip to 2¼″ from SEAM.

5. ASSEMBLE: Stitch border units to block row, brown triangles facing as shown. Press. Stitch upper background to Topper. Press.

6. FINISH: Cut backing to same size as batting. Use your favorite layering and quilting methods. Bind with ⅜″ seam allowance.

Bear Tracks

TOPPER

Photo on page 18.

Use fabric with 42″ usable width. When strips appear in cutting list, cut crossgrain strips (selvage to selvage).

	T	D/Q/K
Size	44x44″	62x62″
Yardage		
Turquoise #1	½ yd	½ yd
Turquoise #2	⅙ yd	⅝ yd
Green	⅝ yd	⅝ yd
Purple #1	⅙ yd	⅙ yd
Purple #2	⅓ yd	⅔ yd
Black #1	⅞ yd	1⅞ yd
Black #2	⅙ yd	⅝ yd
Backing	3 yd	4⅛ yd
Binding	½ yd	⅝ yd
Batting	48x48″	68x68″

Cutting	*Cut in HALF diagonally	T	D/Q/K
Turquoise #1	3½″ square - center square	1	1
	3½x9½″ - center sq border	8	8
Turquoise #2	*3⅞″ squares - paw units	8	8
	2″ strips - Border 3	-	6
Green	3½x9½″ - center square	4	4
	3½″ strips - Border 1	4	4
Purple #1	3½″ squares - center sq border	8	8
Purple #2	3½″ squares - paw units	4	4
	*3⅞″ squares - paw units, Border 2	8	36
Black #1	6½″ squares - paw units	4	4
	*20″ squares - large triangles	2	2
	5″ strips - Border 4	-	6
Black #2	3½″ squares - Borders 1 & 2	4	8
	*3⅞″ squares - Border 2	-	28
	coping pieces 3½x__″ see Step 5	-	4
Binding	2½″ strips	5	7

Directions

Use ¼″ seam allowance.

1. PAW UNITS: Make 16 half-square triangle units with purple #2 and turquoise #2. Make 4 paw units as shown. Press.
2. CENTER SQUARE: Stitch paw units together as shown with green rectangles and turquoise #1 square. Press. Make 4 border units with turquoise #1 rectangles and purple #1 squares. Stitch to sides of center square as shown. Press.
3. LARGE CORNER TRIANGLES: Stitch large black #1 triangles to sides of center square. Press.
4. BORDER 1: Stitch green strips together end to end. Cut 4 borders to fit sides of Topper. Stitch borders to opposite sides of Topper. Stitch black #2 squares to ends of remaining borders. Stitch to remaining sides of Topper. Press. Twin size is finished at this point. Skip to Step 8.
5. BORDER 2: Make 56 half-square triangle units with black #2 and purple #2 triangles. Press. Arrange and stitch half-square triangle units together as shown. Determine width of coping pieces needed, including seam allowance, to make borders fit Topper. Cut and stitch coping

Continued on page 29.

D/Q/K SIZE

See page 37 for quilted pillowcase directions.

Folk Art Fantasy
TOPPER

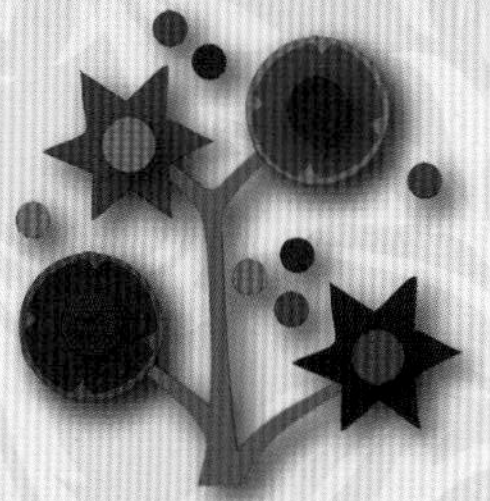

Photo on page 20.

Use fabric with 42″ usable width. When strips appear in cutting list, cut crossgrain strips (selvage to selvage).

Patterns are given for fusible web applique, reversed and ready to be traced. Be sure to have plenty of fusible web on hand if using this method. Reverse patterns and add seam allowance if doing hand applique.

Size	52 x 52″

Yardage

Dark blue	2¼ yd
Reds #1- #2	1 yd each
Red #3	¼ yd
Teal	⅝ yd
Medium blue	⅙ yd
Greens	⅛ yd each of 3
Backing	3⅜ yd
Binding	⅝ yd
Batting	56 x 56″

Cutting
Patterns on pages 42-44

Dark blue	center square	1 square 18½″
	pieced corner units	4 squares 13″
	large corner triangles	*2 squares 20⅞″
	blue border	6 strips 2½″ wide
Red #1	narrow red border	2 pieces 1½ x 18½″
		2 pieces 1½ x 20½″
	red squares border	22 squares 4½″
	appliques as desired	
Red #2	red squares border	22 squares 4½″
	appliques as desired	
Red #3	appliques as desired	
Teal	pieced corner units	4 squares 2½″
		8 pieces 2½ x 13″
	tree trunk	1
Med blue	flower center	1
Greens	leaves as desired	
Binding	2½″ strips	6

*Cut in HALF diagonally

Directions

Use ¼″ seam allowance.

1. **PIECED CORNER UNITS:** Make 4 units as shown. Cut in half diagonally.

2. **CENTER SQUARE:** Stitch short red border pieces to opposite sides of center square. Stitch long red border pieces to remaining sides. Press. Stitch pieced corner units to center square. Press.

3. **APPLIQUE:** Applique center square as shown. Applique large blue triangles as shown, placing lower edge of design 2″ from raw edge of long side of triangle.

4. **LARGE CORNER TRIANGLES:** Stitch large blue triangles to sides of center square. Press.

5. **RED SQUARES BORDER:** Stitch 10 red squares together for each side. Stitch 12 red squares together for top and bottom. Press. Stitch side borders to Topper, then top and bottom borders. Press.

6. **BLUE BORDER:** Stitch border strips together to fit sides of Topper. Make 2. Stitch to sides of Topper. Repeat at top and bottom. Press.

7. **FINISH:** Piece backing to same size as batting. Use your favorite layering and quilting methods. Bind with ⅜″ seam allowance.

See page 7 for quilted pillowcase directions.

1.

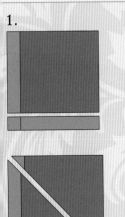

2-3.

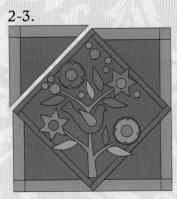

3-4.

Diagrams continued on page 25.

Amish Puzzle
TOPPER

Photo on page 22.
Use fabric with 42″ usable width. When strips appear in cutting list, cut crossgrain strips (selvage to selvage).

	T	D/Q/K
Size	42×42″	66×66″
12″ blocks	9	25

Yardage

	T	D/Q/K
Light purple	1 yd	2⅜ yd
Gold, rust, teal, light olive, dark olive	⅝ yd ea of 3	⅝ yd ea of 5
Dark purple	⅝ yd	⅞ yd
Backing	2⅞ yd	4¼ yd
Binding	½ yd	⅝ yd
Batting	46×46″	72×72″

Cutting

*Cut in HALF diagonally

		T	D/Q/K
Light purple	*9⅞″ squares - blocks	5	13
	*3⅞″ squares - blocks	32	88
From each of other block fabrics:			
	*9⅞″ squares - blocks	2	3
	*3⅞″ squares - blocks	11	18
Dark purple	3½″ strips - border	4	7
Binding	2½″ strips	5	7

Directions

Use ¼″ seam allowance.

1. BLOCKS: Make [T 9] [D/Q/K 25] blocks as shown. Press.

2. ROWS: Stitch blocks into [T 3 rows of 3] [D/Q/K 5 rows of 5] as shown. Press. Stitch rows together. Press.

3. BORDER: Cut, or stitch border strips together to same length as Topper. Make 2. Stitch to sides of Topper. Repeat at top and bottom. Press.

4. FINISH: Piece backing to same size as batting. Use your favorite layering and quilting methods. Bind with ⅜″ seam allowance.

1. For each block:

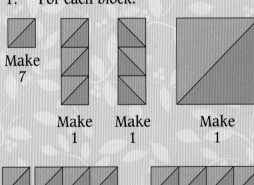

Make 7

Make 1   Make 1   Make 1

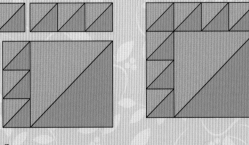

2.

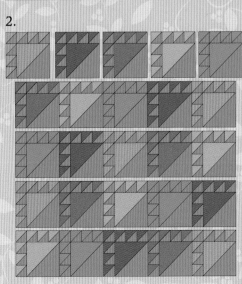

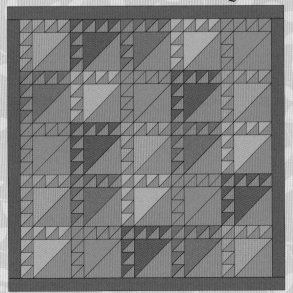

D/Q/K SIZE

23

Amish Puzzle
PILLOW TOPPER

Photo on page 22.

Use fabric with 42″ usable width. When strips appear in cutting list, cut crossgrain strips (selvage to selvage).

	T	D/Q	K
Size	55 x 40″	72 x 40″	89 x 40″
12″ blocks	3	4	5

Yardage

	T	D/Q	K
Light purple	½ yd	½ yd	⅝ yd
Choose from:			
Gold, rust, teal, light olive, dark olive	⅜ yd ea of 3	⅜ yd ea of 4	⅜ yd ea of 5
Dark purple	1⅛ yd	1⅝ yd	1⅝ yd
Teal	1⅝ yd	2⅛ yd	2⅝ yd
Backing	1⅞ yd	2⅓ yd	2⅞ yd
Binding	½ yd	⅝ yd	⅝ yd
Batting	59 x 44″	76 x 44″	93 x 44″

Cutting

		T	D/Q	K
Light purple	*9⅞″ squares	2	2	3
	*3⅞″ squares	11	14	18
From each of other block fabrics:				
	*9⅞″ squares	1	1	1
	*3⅞″ squares	4	4	4
Dark purple	**18¼″ squares - side triangles	1	2	2
	*9⅜″ squares - corner triangles	2	2	2
	2½″ strips - border & sashing	6	8	9
Teal	upper bkgrnd	17½x51½″	17½x68½″	17½x85½″
Binding	2½″ strips	5	6	7

*Cut in HALF diagonally   **Cut in QUARTERS diagonally

Directions

Use ¼″ seam allowance.

1. BLOCKS: Make [T 3] [D/Q 4] [K 5] blocks as shown in diagrams on page 23. Press.

2. BLOCK ROW: Arrange blocks and setting triangles as shown. Stitch blocks and setting triangles into diagonal rows. Press. Stitch rows together. Press.

3. SASHING & UPPER BACKGROUND: Piece sashing to width of Topper. Stitch to top of block row. Press. Trim upper background piece to width of Topper and stitch to sashing strip. Press.

4. BORDER: Cut or stitch border strips together to same width as Topper. Make 2. Stitch to top and bottom. Repeat at sides. Press.

5. FINISH: Cut backing to same size as batting. Use your favorite layering and quilting methods. Bind with ⅜″ seam allowance.

2.

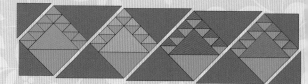

D/Q SIZE

24

BLUE DAHLIA TOPPER
Continued from page 9

FOLK ART FANTASY TOPPER
Continued from page 21

2. For each star block:

Make
4

5.

3. For each side setting triangle:

Make
2

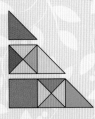

4. For each corner setting triangle:

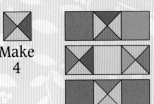

Make
1

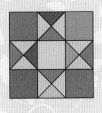

6.

5.

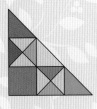

25

Holiday Pines
PILLOW TOPPER

Photo on page 26.

Use fabric with 42″ usable width. When strips appear in cutting list, cut crossgrain strips (selvage to selvage) unless otherwise noted.

	T	D/Q	K
Size	48 x 40″	70 x 40″	88 x 40″
12″ tree blocks	2	3	4
12″ star blocks	1	2	3

Yardage

Green #1	1⅝ yd	2¼ yd	2¾ yd
Greens - 4 fabrics	⅙ yd ea	¼ yd ea	⅓ yd ea
Reds - #1 - #4	⅙ yd ea	⅓ yd ea	⅓ yd ea
Blues - #1 & #2	⅜ yd ea	½ yd ea	⅝ yd ea
Yellow	⅙ yd	⅙ yd	⅙ yd
Tan	⅛ yd	⅛ yd	⅛ yd
Backing	1⅝ yd	2¼ yd	2¾ yd
Binding	½ yd	⅝ yd	⅝ yd
Batting	52 x 44″	74 x 44″	92 x 44″

Cutting *Cut in QUARTERS diagonally

Green #1				
upper bkgrnd	48½ x 18½″	70½ x 18½″	88½ x 18½″
2 side rectangles	6½ x 16½″	5½ x 16½″	2½ x 16½″
2½″ strips cut lengthwise	3	3	3
Greens #s in chart are totals from the 4 fabrics			
tree blocks			
3½ x 6½″	2	3	4
3½ x 8½″	2	3	4
3½ x 10½″	2	3	4
1½″ squares	16	24	32
star blocks			
1½″ squares	8	16	24
*3¼″ squares	2	4	6
Red #1 tree blocks			
1½″ squares	20	30	40
2½″ squares	4	6	8
Red #2 star blocks			
1½″ squares	20	40	60
2½″ squares	1	2	3
Reds #1-#4 squares border			
2½″ squares	12 each	18 each	22 each
Blue #1 tree blocks			
1½ x 2½″	16	24	32
2½ x 3½″	4	6	8
3½ x 4″	4	6	8
3½ x 4½″	8	12	16
Blue #2 star blocks			
1½ x 6½″	4	8	12
1½ x 8½″	4	8	12
1½ x 10½″	4	8	12
Yellow star blocks			
*3¼″ squares	2	4	6
Tan tree blocks			
1½ x 3½″	2	3	4
Binding 2½″ strips	5	6	7

Directions

Use ¼″ seam allowance.

1. TREE BLOCKS: (for each block)

   a. Corner Units: Make 4 four-patches with 1½″ squares as shown. Add 1½ x 2½″ blue pieces as shown. Press.

   b. Trunk Units: Make 1 trunk unit as shown using tan piece and 3½ x 4″ blue pieces. Press.

   c. Row 2: Make 2 units as shown with 1½″ squares, 2½″ squares, and 1½ x 2½″ pieces. Press. Stitch to each end of 3½ x 8½″ green piece as shown. Trim seam allowances to ¼″ and press.

   d. Row 1: Stitch 3½ x 4½″ blue pieces to each end of 3½ x 6½″ green pieces as shown. Trim and press.

   e. Row 3: Repeat Step 1d with 3½ x 4½″ blue pieces and 3½ x 10½″ green pieces.

   f. Assemble block in horizontal rows as shown. Press.

2. STAR BLOCKS: (for each block)

   a. Make 4 four-patches with 1½″ squares as shown. Press.

   b. Make 4 quarter-square triangle units with triangles cut from 3¼″ squares. Press.

   c. Assemble star in horizontal rows as shown. Press.

   d. Stitch 6½″ blue strips to sides. Stitch 1½″ red squares to 6½″ blue strips as shown and stitch to top and bottom. Repeat for two more rounds using 8½″ strips and 10½″ strips. Press.

3. SQUARES BORDER: Stitch red squares into two borders of [T 24] [D/Q 35] [K 44] squares each. Adjust seams if needed to make borders the same width as upper background [T 48½″] [D/Q 70½″] [K 88½″]. Press.

Continued on page 28.

For each tree block:

1a. 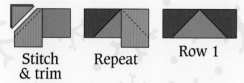 Make 4   Make 2   Make 2

1b. Make 1

1c. Row 2

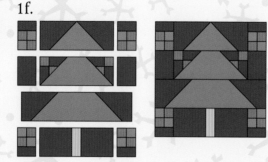

Make 2   Stitch   Trim   Press   Repeat

1d. Row 1

Stitch & trim   Repeat   Row 1

1e. Row 3   1f.

For each star block:

2a. Make 4   2c.   2d.

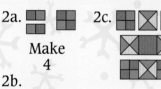 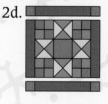 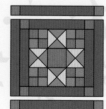

2b.

Make 4

3-4.

Side Rectangle   Side Rectangle

Continued from page 27

4. ASSEMBLE

  a. Stitch blocks into a row, alternating trees and stars. Press.

  b. Measure width of row. Cut 2 green #1 strips that measurement. Stitch to top and bottom of block row. Press.

  c. Add side rectangles to ends of row to make it the same width as upper background [T 48½″] [D/Q 70½″] [K 88½″].

  d. Stitch squares borders to top and bottom. Press.

  e. Measure width of Topper. Cut remaining green #1 strip that measurement. Stitch to bottom of Topper. Press.

  f. Stitch upper background to top. Press.

5. FINISH: Cut backing to same size as batting. Use your favorite layering and quilting methods. Bind with ⅜″ seam allowance.

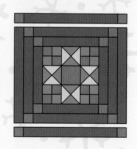

Quilt
Directions for squares quilt are on page 3.

D/Q SIZE

1. Make 16

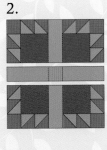
Make 4

2.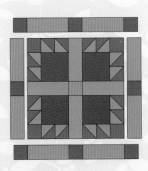

BEAR TRACKS TOPPER
Continued from page 19

pieces to border units. Stitch black #2 squares to ends of 2 of the borders. Stitch borders to Topper as shown. Press.

6. BORDER 3: Piece turquoise #2 strips to same length as Topper. Make 2. Stitch to sides. Press. Repeat at top and bottom. Press.

7. BORDER 4: Repeat Step 6.

8. FINISH: Piece backing to same size as batting. Use your favorite layering and quilting methods. Bind with ⅜″ seam allowance.

3.

4.

5.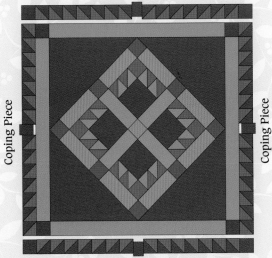

Coping Piece

Coping Piece

Coping Piece

Coping Piece

Coping Piece

6.

7.

Christmas Tree Lot
PILLOW TOPPER

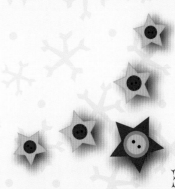

Photo on page 30.

Use fabric with 42″ usable width. When strips appear in cutting list, cut crossgrain strips (selvage to selvage).

Patterns are given for fusible web applique, reversed and ready to be traced. Be sure to have plenty of fusible web on hand if using this method. Reverse patterns and add seam allowance if doing hand applique.

		T	D/Q	K
Size		48×40″	70×40″	86×40″
Yardage				
Background	blue	1⅝ yd	2¼ yd	2¾ yd
	white	½ yd	½ yd	⅝ yd
Trees	5-6 greens	⅜ yd ea	½ yd ea	½ yd ea
Tree trunks	1-2 browns	⅛ yd ea	⅛ yd ea	⅛ yd ea
Tree ornaments	3-6 fabrics	⅛ yd ea	⅛ yd ea	⅛ yd ea
Backing		1¾ yd	2⅜ yd	2¾ yd
Binding		½ yd	⅝ yd	⅝ yd
Batting		52×44″	74×44″	90×44″

Cutting Patterns on pages 51-53

Background		T	D/Q	K
blue		48½ x 34½″	70½ x 34½″	86½ x 34½″
white	6½″ strips	2	2	3
Strip-set trees	1½″ strips	1 total	2 total	2 total
	2″ strips	1 total	2 total	2 total
	2½″ strips	2 total	4 total	4 total
	3″ strips	2 total	4 total	4 total
Plain trees		1	1-2	2-3
Other appliques as desired				
Binding	2½″ strips	5	6	7

Directions

Use ¼″ seam allowance.

1. BACKGROUND: Stitch 6½″ white strips end to end. Cut [T 48½″] [D/Q 70½″] [K 86½″] long. Stitch to bottom of background. Press.

2. STRIP SETS FOR TREES: For T, stitch the 6 strips for trees in any order. Apply fusible web and cut out 6 trees. For D/Q and K, make 2 strip sets. Cut out 8 pieced trees for D/Q and 9 pieced trees for K. Press.

3. APPLIQUE: Arrange pieces as shown in diagram for twin size. For double/queen and king, place extra trees as desired. Embellish trees with stars and ornaments. Use rick-rack or fabric pieces cut with wavy rotary blade or wavy scissors to make garland trim for trees.

4. FINISH: Cut backing to same size as batting. Use your favorite layering and quilting methods. Bind with ⅜″ seam allowance. Optional: Try glow-in-the-dark thread or decorative threads to quilt the snowflakes.

TWIN SIZE

Be Mine
PILLOW TOPPER

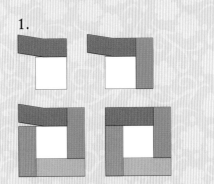

Photo on page 32.

Use fabric with 42″ usable width. When strips appear in cutting list, cut crossgrain strips (selvage to selvage).

Patterns are given for fusible web applique, reversed and ready to be traced. Be sure to have plenty of fusible web on hand if using this method. Reverse patterns and add seam allowance if doing hand applique.

		T	D/Q	K
Size		48×40″	70×40″	88×40″
12″ blocks		4	5	7

Yardage

	T	D/Q	K
Dark red	1⅝ yd	2¼ yd	2¾ yd
Reds - ¼ yd each	5 or more	6 or more	8 or more
Pinks - ¼ yd each	3 or more	4 or more	6 or more
White	¾ yd	⅞ yd	1¼ yd
Backing	1⅝ yd	2¼ yd	2¾ yd
Binding	½ yd	⅝ yd	⅝ yd
Batting	52×44″	74×44″	92×44″

Cutting   Patterns on page 50

		T	D/Q	K
Dark red	upper bkgrnd	48½×20½″	70½×20½″	88½×20½″
	side rectangles			
	5½×12½″	-	2	-
	2½×12½″	-	-	2
All reds & pinks	blocks			
	4½×12″	16	20	28
	patchwork bdr			
	2½″ squares	24	36	44
	hearts	4 sets	5 sets	7 sets
White	blocks			
	8″ squares	4	5	7
	border			
	2½″ strips	3	4	5
	patchwork bdr			
	2½″ squares	24	34	44
Binding	2½″ strips	5	6	7

Directions

Use ¼″ seam allowance.

1. **BLOCKS:** Make [T 4] [D/Q 5] [K 7] blocks. Stitch first rectangle partway across center square as shown, finishing seam after other rectangles are added. Press. Applique hearts to blocks. Place 12½″ ruler or template on right side of block, tilted to left as shown. Corners of ruler or template should meet edges of block. Cut [T 2] [D/Q 2] [K 3] blocks. Repeat for other [T 2] [D/Q 3] [K 4] blocks, tilting ruler or template to right.

2. **ASSEMBLE:** Stitch blocks into a row as shown. If required, stitch side rectangles to ends of block row. Stitch white strips together and cut to same length as block row. Stitch to Topper. Make two patchwork borders alternating reds and pinks with white. Stitch to Topper. Stitch upper background to top. Press.

3. **FINISH:** Cut backing to same size as batting. Use your favorite layering and quilting methods. Bind with ⅜″ seam allowance.

1.

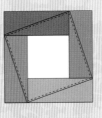

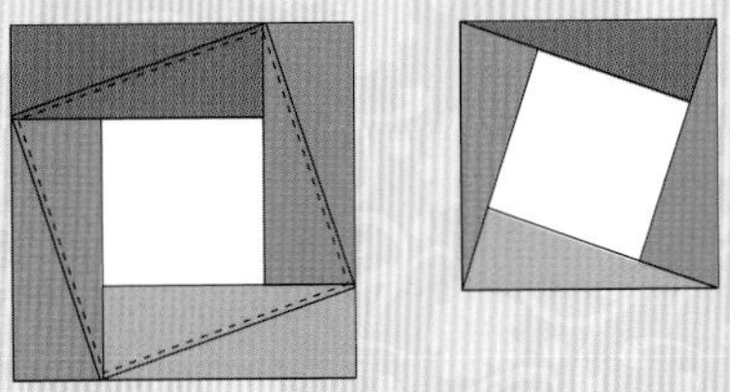

Cut with ruler tilted to left:
T - 2
D/Q - 2
K - 3

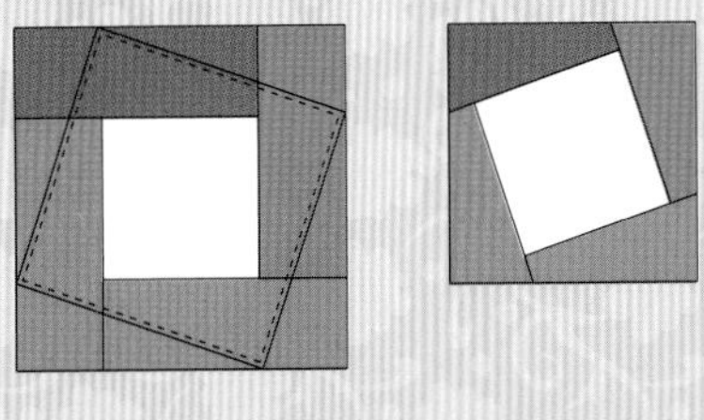

Cut with ruler tilted to right:
T - 2
D/Q - 3
K - 4

D/Q SIZE

Quilt

Directions for squares quilt are on page 3.

33

Celebrate!
PILLOW TOPPER

Photo on page 34.

Use fabric with 42″ usable width. When strips appear in cutting list, cut crossgrain strips (selvage to selvage).

Patterns are given for fusible web applique, reversed and ready to be traced. Be sure to have plenty of fusible web on hand if using this method. Reverse patterns and add seam allowance if doing hand applique.

Note: Pillow Topper in photo is a queen size photographed on a twin bed. It was made to be the same width as the twin quilt in the photo.

Directions

Use ¼″ seam allowance.

1. BACKGROUND: Stitch green 3½″ strips end to end. Cut into 2 segments [T 48½″] [D/Q 70½″] [K 86½″]. Stitch to top and bottom of 18½″ blue piece. Stitch 16½″ blue piece to top. Press.

2. APPLIQUE: Place pieces as shown in diagram for queen size. For twin, condense the design and/or eliminate a few pieces. For king, spread the design and/or add a few pieces.

3. QUILT: Cut backing to same size as batting. Layer and quilt as desired. Trim backing and batting even with top.

4. PRAIRIE POINTS & FACING:

   a. Fold and press prairie points for edging as shown.

   b. Pin and then baste prairie points to side edges of Topper, slipping one inside the other if needed to space them evenly.

   c. Measure sides of Topper and cut 2 facing strips that length. Press in half lengthwise, wrong sides together. Stitch to sides of Topper matching all raw edges. Fold to back of quilt so prairie points extend at edge. Hand stitch folded edge to back of quilt. Facing will be ¾″ wide.

   d. Repeat Step 4c at top and bottom of Topper but add ½″ at each end. Fold facing to back of quilt and turn under extensions. Hand stitch in place.

		T	D/Q	K
Size		48x40″	70x40″	86x40″
Yardage				
Prairie points, gift boxes, hats, balloons				
5 fabrics		¼ yd ea	¼ yd ea	¼ yd ea
Other appliques				
4 fabrics		⅛ yd ea	⅛ yd ea	⅛ yd ea
Background	blue	1⅝ yd	2¼ yd	2¾ yd
	green	½ yd	⅝ yd	⅝ yd
Backing		1⅝ yd	2¼ yd	2¾ yd
Facing		½ yd	½ yd	⅝ yd
Batting		52x44″	74x44″	90x44″
Cutting Patterns on pages 44-47				
Prairie points - 4½″ squares		20	20	20
Gift boxes - 5x8½″		2	2	2
Ribbons - ¾x5″		2	2	2
	¾x8½″	1	1	1
Large candles - 1¼x8″		3	3	3
Other appliques as desired				
Background				
blue		48½x16½″	70½x16½″	86½x16½″
		48½x18½″	70½x18½″	86½x18½″
green	3½″ strips	3	4	5
Facing - 2″ strips		5	6	7

4a.

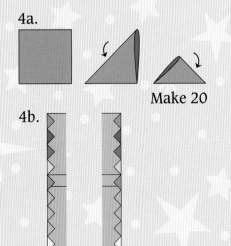

Make 20

4b.

D/Q SIZE

Celebrate!
TOPPER

Photo on page 34.

Use fabric with 42″ usable width. When strips appear in cutting list, cut crossgrain strips (selvage to selvage).

NOTE: Ample yardage given for any color sequence.

	T	D/Q	K
Size	72x72″	90x90″	106x106″
Yardage			
Brights - 6 fabrics	1⅛ yd ea	1½ yd ea	2 yd ea
Backing	4⅝ yd	8⅜ yd	9¾ yd
Binding	⅔ yd	⅞ yd	⅞ yd
Batting	78x78″	96x96″	112x112″
Cutting			
Brights - 3½″ strips of each fabric	9	13	18
Binding - 2½″ strips	8	10	11

Directions

Use ¼″ seam allowance.

1. CENTER PANEL: Starting with center square, maintaining chosen color sequence, and piecing strips end to end where needed, stitch and trim strips of next color to two opposite sides, then to remaining two sides. Press. Continue for a total of 8 rounds for twin, 10 rounds for double/queen, and 12 rounds for king (count 1st set of strips sewn to center square as Round 1).

1.
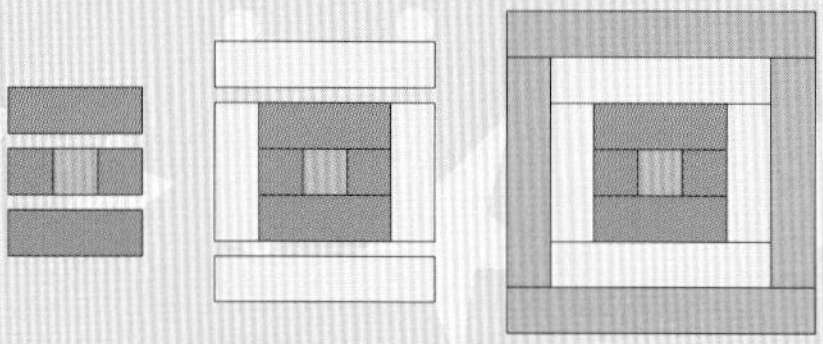

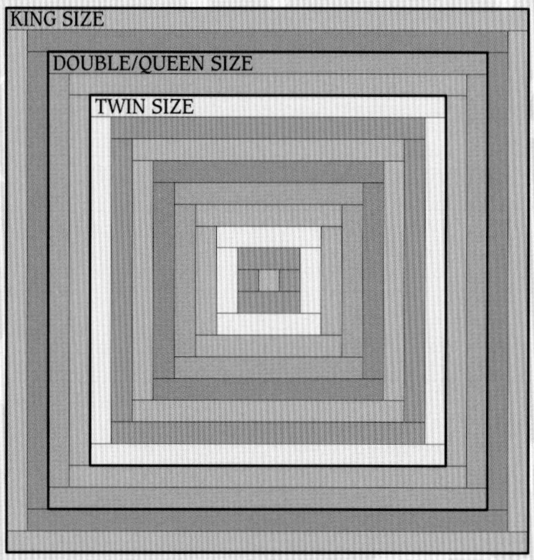

2.
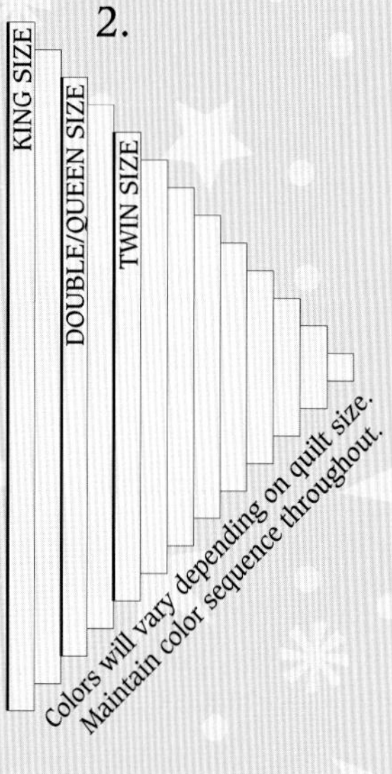

2. CORNER UNITS: Piecing strips end to end when needed, prepare 4 sets of strips the following lengths

	T	D/Q	K
Row 1	51½″	63½″	75½″
Row 2	45½″	57½″	69½″
Row 3	39½″	51½″	63½″
Row 4	33½″	45½″	57½″
Row 5	27½″	39½″	51½″
Row 6	21½″	33½″	45½″
Row 7	15½″	27½″	39½″
Row 8	9½″	21½″	33½″
Row 9	3½″	15½″	27½″
Row 10	-	9½″	21½″
Row 11	-	3½″	15½″
Row 12	-	-	9½″
Row 13	-	-	3½″

Fold each strip in half to find center and stitch corner unit as shown. Press. Make 4. Stitch a corner unit to each side of center panel. Press. To control stretching, trim points of corner units with batting and backing *after* quilting.

3. FINISH: Piece backing to same size as batting. Use your favorite layering and quilting methods. Bind with ⅜″ seam allowance. Topper in photo was machine quilted in a 3″ diagonal grid which makes it look as though it is made of 3″ squares.

KING SIZE
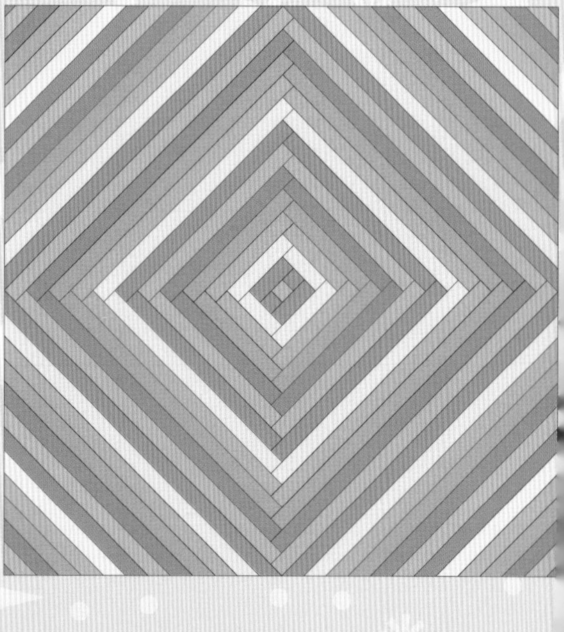

Bear Tracks
QUILTED PILLOWCASE

Photo on page 18.

Standard Size: 20 x 30″

Use fabric with 42″ usable width. When strips appear in cutting list, cut crossgrain strips (selvage to selvage).

Yardage for 1 pillowcase

Main fabric	1 yd
Patchwork	¼ yd each of 4 fabrics
Lining	1½ yd
Batting	33 x 46″

Cutting *Cut in HALF diagonally

Main fabric	21½ x 42½″
	1 strip 3½″ wide
Binding	1 strip 2½″ wide
Patchwork	1 strip 2″ wide of color 1
	1 strip 2″ wide of color 2
	*7 squares 3⅞″ of color 3
	*7 squares 3⅞″ of color 4

Directions

Use ¼″ seam allowance unless otherwise noted.

1. PATCHWORK: Make 14 half-square triangle units as shown. Stitch into a row. Press.

2. ASSEMBLE: Stitch 2″ strips to each side of patchwork row. Stitch 3½″ main fabric strip to one side and large main fabric piece to other side. Press.

3. FINISH: Cut lining to same size as batting. Layer and quilt as desired. Trim backing and batting even with top. Fold pillowcase in half lengthwise, right sides together. Leaving end with patchwork open, stitch side and end using ⅜″ seam allowance. Turn right side out. Press binding in half lengthwise, wrong sides together and bind edge using ⅜″ seam allowance.

1.

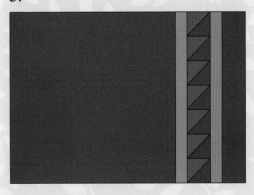

2.

3.

Beary Special Angels
PILLOW TOPPER

Photo on page 38.

Use fabric with 42″ usable width. When strips appear in cutting list, cut crossgrain strips (selvage to selvage) unless otherwise noted.

Patterns are given for fusible web applique, reversed and ready to be traced. Be sure to have plenty of fusible web on hand if using this method. Reverse patterns and add seam allowance if doing hand applique.

		T	D/Q	K
Size		48x40″	70x40″	86x40″
Yardage				
Background	blue	1⅝ yd	2¼ yd	2¾ yd
	green	⅙ yd	⅙ yd	¼ yd
Appliques, prairie points	10 fabrics	⅜ yd ea	⅜ yd ea	⅜ yd ea
	black	⅛ yd	⅛ yd	⅛ yd
	2 tans	⅙ yd ea	⅙ yd ea	⅙ yd ea
Backing		1¾ yd	2⅜ yd	2¾ yd
Facing		½ yd	½ yd	⅝ yd
Batting		52x44″	74x44″	90x44″
Cutting Patterns on pages 48-49				
Background blue		48½x37½″	70½x37½″	86½x37½″
	cut lengthwise	2x48½″	2x70½″	2x86½″
green	2″ strips	2	2	3
Appliques	2 girls, 1 boy, hearts, stars			
Prairie points	6¼″ squares	9	13	16
Facing	2″ strips	5	6	7

Directions

Use ¼″ seam allowance.

1. BACKGROUND: Stitch green 2″ strips end to end. Cut green strips to [T 48½″] [D/Q 70½″] [K 86½″] long. Stitch green strip to bottom of background. Stitch blue strip to green strip. Press.

2. APPLIQUE: Place pieces as shown in diagram for twin size. For double/queen and king, spread the design and/or add a few stars.

3. QUILT: Cut backing to same size as batting. Layer and quilt as desired. Trim backing and batting even with top.

4. PRAIRIE POINTS & FACING:

   a. Fold and press prairie points for edging as shown.

   b. Pin and then baste prairie points to bottom edge of Topper, slipping one inside the other if needed to space them evenly.

   c. Measure top and bottom of Topper and piece 2 facing strips to that length. Press in half lengthwise, wrong sides together. Stitch to top and bottom of Topper, matching all raw edges. Fold to back of Topper so prairie points extend at edge. Hand stitch folded edge to back of Topper. Facing will be ¾″ wide.

   d. Repeat Step 4c at sides of Topper, adding ½″ at each end. Fold facing to back of Topper and turn under extensions. Hand stitch in place.

TWIN SIZE

4a.

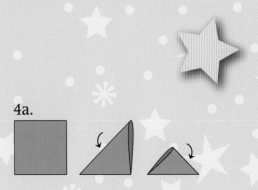

39

Beary Special Angels
QUILT

Photo on page 38.

Use fabric with 42″ usable width. When strips appear in cutting list, cut crossgrain strips (selvage to selvage).

		T	D/Q	K
Size		72 x 88″	96 x 96″	104 x 96″
8″ squares		99	144	156

Yardage

		T	D/Q	K
Blocks, binding	11 fabrics	1 yd ea	1¼ yd ea	1¼ yd ea
Prairie points	4 or more fabrics	⅓ yd ea	⅓ yd ea	⅓ yd ea
Backing		5⅝ yd	8⅞ yd	8⅞ yd
Batting		78 x 94″	102 x 102″	110 x 102″

Cutting

		T	D/Q	K
Blocks	8½″ squares	99	144	156
Prairie points	8½″ squares	5	5	6
	4½″ squares	8	8	10
	3¼″ squares	6	9	9
	2½″ squares	16	16	16
Binding	2½″ strips from each of 11 fabrics	1-2	1-2	1-2

Directions

Use ¼″ seam allowance.

1. PRAIRIE POINTS: Fold and press all squares for prairie points as shown. Group into sets of one 8½″, two 4½″, three 3¼″, and four 2½″.

2. ASSEMBLE:

   a. Arrange squares into:

      Twin - 11 horizontal rows of 9
      D/Q - 12 horizontal rows of 12
      King - 12 horizontal rows of 13

   b. Pin sets of prairie points on squares in positions desired, orienting them as shown in diagram.

   c. Stitch squares into rows, catching prairie points in seams. Press seam allowances of odd rows to left and seam allowances of even rows to right.

   d. Stitch rows together, catching prairie points in seams. Press.

3. FINISH: Piece backing vertically to same size as batting. Layer and quilt as desired. Subcut binding strips into pieces from 6-12″ long. Stitch binding pieces end to end in random order. Press seam allowances open. Press in half lengthwise, wrong sides together and bind quilt using ⅜″ seam allowance.

1.
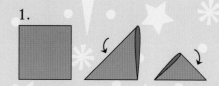

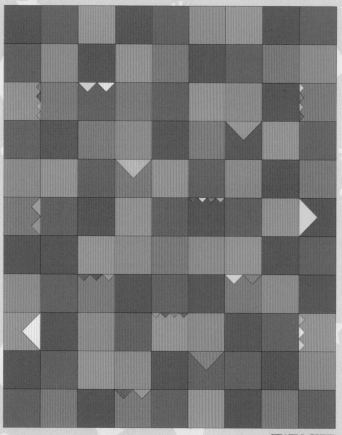

TWIN SIZE

Sherbet Stars
QUILTED PILLOWCASE

Photo on page 12. Standard Size: 20 x 30″

Use fabric with 42″ usable width. When strips appear in cutting list, cut crossgrain strips (selvage to selvage).

6″ blocks	7

Yardage for 1 pillowcase
Main fabric	¾ yd
Block background	⅜ yd
Stars, border, binding	¼ yd each of 7-14 fabrics
Lining	1½ yd
Batting	33 x 46″

Cutting
	*Cut in HALF diagonally
Main fabric	24 x 42½″
Block background	28 squares 2″
	*28 squares 2⅜″
Stars 7 sets of	*4 squares 2⅜″
	7 squares 3½″
Border, binding	1 strip 2¾″ wide of each star fabric

Directions

Use ¼″ seam allowance unless otherwise noted.

1. BLOCKS: Make 7 blocks using diagrams on page 13. Stitch into a row. Press.

2. BORDER/BINDING: Subcut border/binding strips into pieces 2½-4½″ long. Stitch pieces end to end in random order to a length of approximately 88″. Press seam allowances open. Cut into 2 pieces 42½″ long. Trim one to 1″ wide for border. Save 2¾″-wide piece for binding.

3. ASSEMBLE: Stitch border to 42½″ side of main fabric. Stitch row of blocks to other side of border. Press.

4. FINISH: Cut lining to same size as batting. Layer and quilt as desired. Trim backing and batting along block edge to ¼″ from raw edge of block row (this leaves a total of ½″ of batting to fill the wide binding). Trim remaining sides even with top. Fold pillowcase in half lengthwise, right sides together. Leaving end with patchwork open, stitch side and end using ⅜″ seam allowance. Turn right side out. Press binding in half lengthwise, wrong sides together. Match raw edges of binding to raw edge of block row. Stitch ¼″ from raw edges. Turn to inside and hand stitch in place.

2-3.

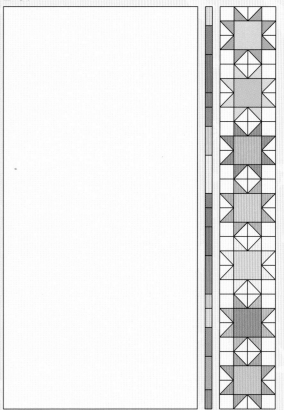

4.

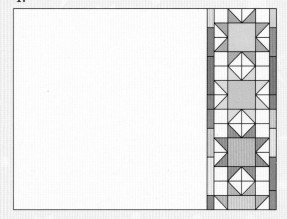

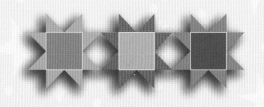

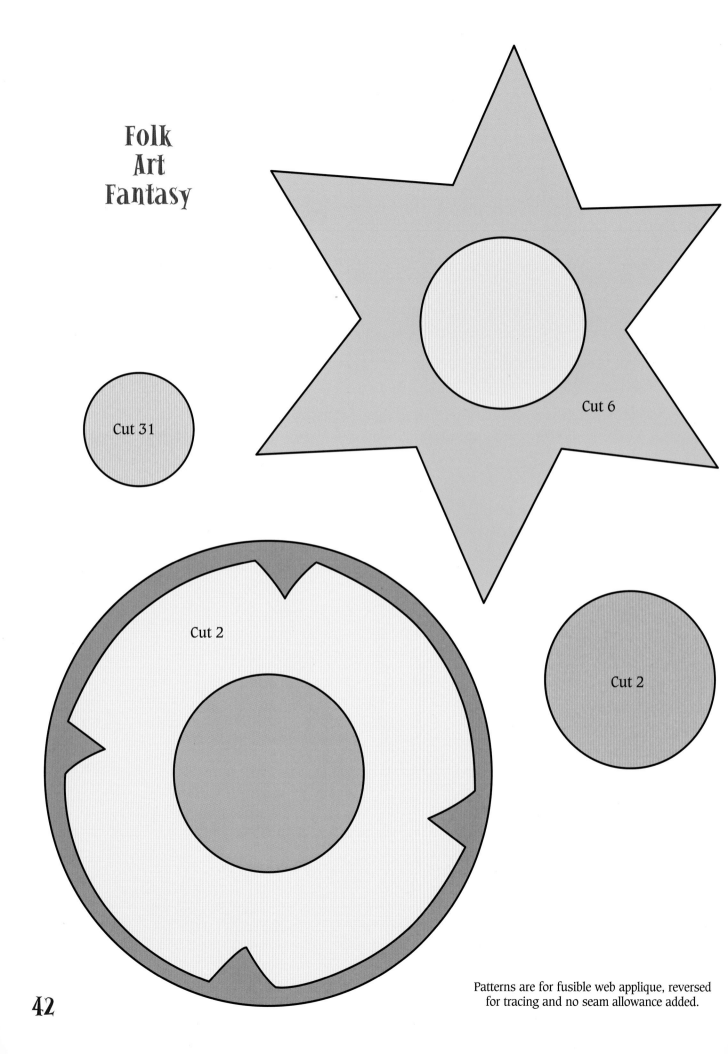

Folk
Art
Fantasy

Cut 31

Cut 6

Cut 2

Cut 2

Patterns are for fusible web applique, reversed
for tracing and no seam allowance added.

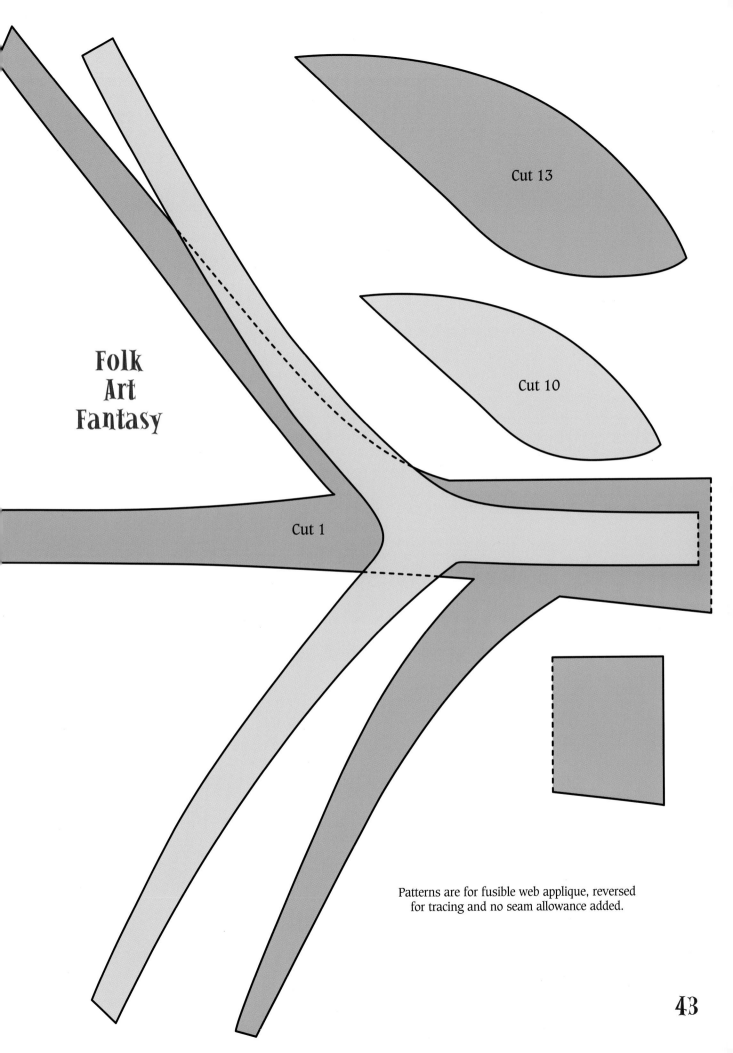

Folk
Art
Fantasy

Cut 13

Cut 10

Cut 1

Patterns are for fusible web applique, reversed
for tracing and no seam allowance added.

43

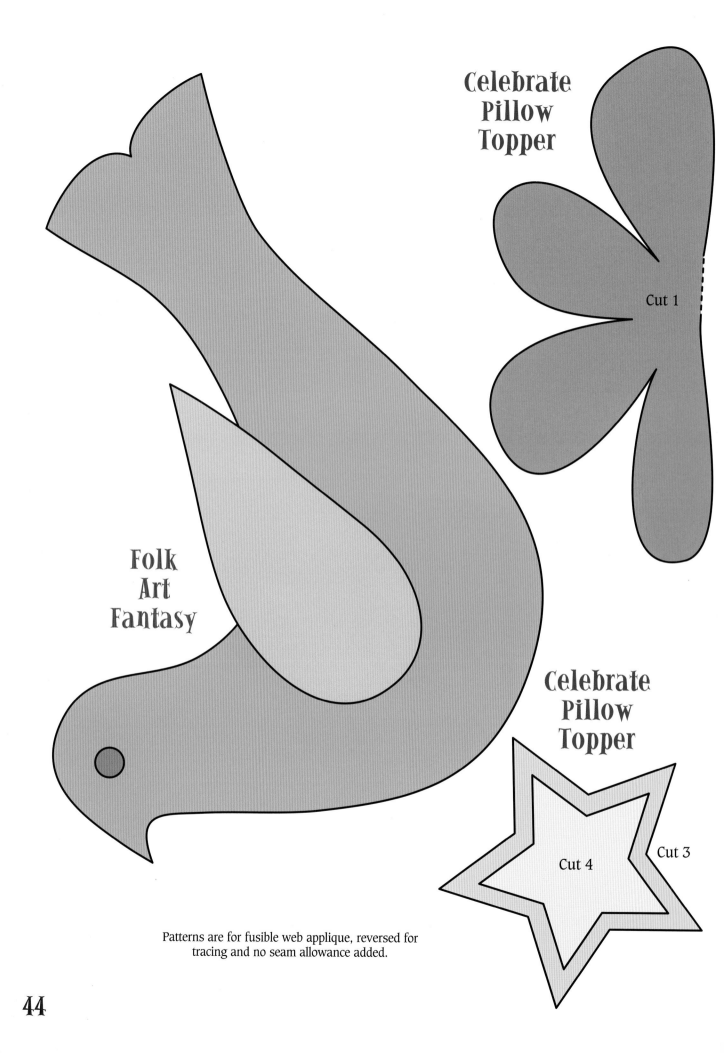

Celebrate
Pillow
Topper

Cut 1

Folk
Art
Fantasy

Celebrate
Pillow
Topper

Cut 4

Cut 3

Patterns are for fusible web applique, reversed for
tracing and no seam allowance added.

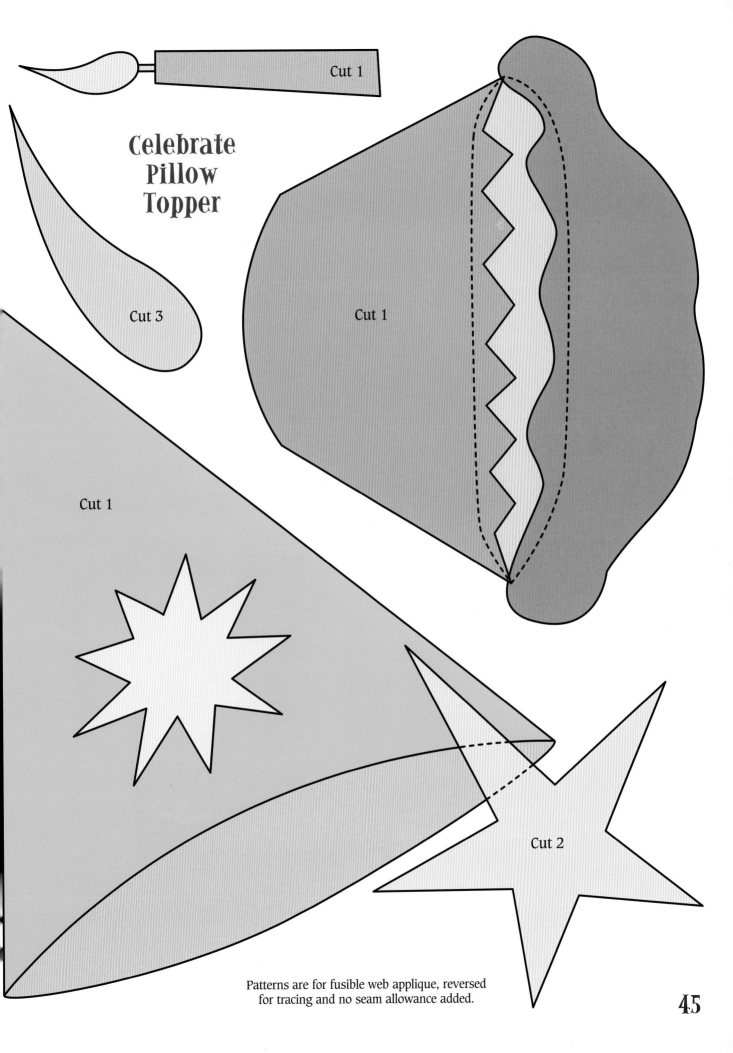

Cut 1

Celebrate
Pillow
Topper

Cut 3

Cut 1

Cut 1

Cut 2

Patterns are for fusible web applique, reversed
for tracing and no seam allowance added.

Celebrate Pillow Topper

Cut 1

Cut 1

Cut 1

Cut 1

Cut 2

Patterns are for fusible web applique, reversed for tracing and no seam allowance added.

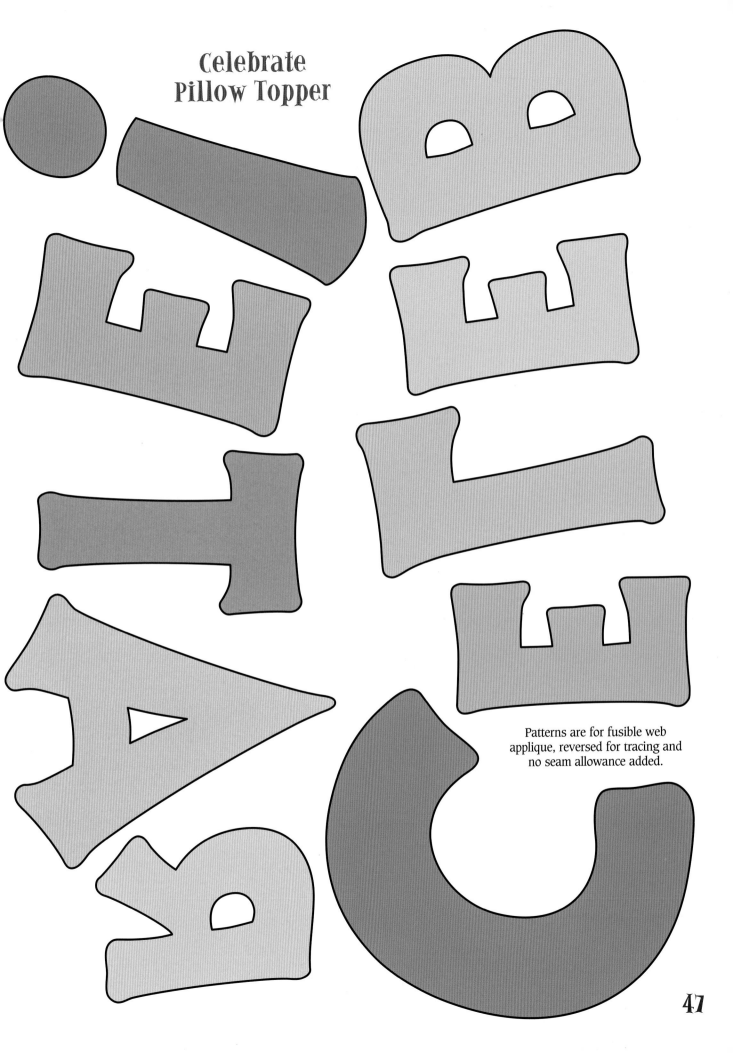

Celebrate
Pillow Topper

Patterns are for fusible web applique, reversed for tracing and no seam allowance added.

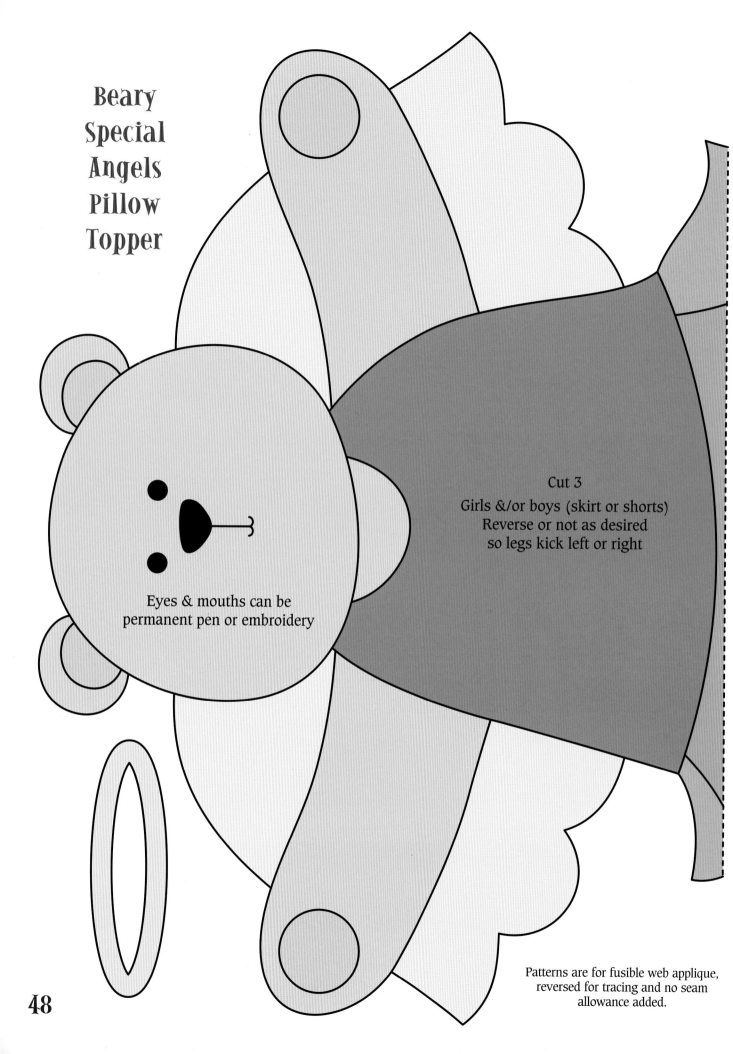

Beary Special Angels Pillow Topper

Eyes & mouths can be permanent pen or embroidery

Cut 3
Girls &/or boys (skirt or shorts)
Reverse or not as desired
so legs kick left or right

Patterns are for fusible web applique,
reversed for tracing and no seam
allowance added.

48

Beary Special Angels Pillow Topper

Cut 3

Girls &/or boys (skirt or shorts)
Reverse or not as desired
so legs kick left or right

Cut number
desired

Patterns are for fusible web applique,
reversed for tracing and no seam
allowance added.

Cut 2

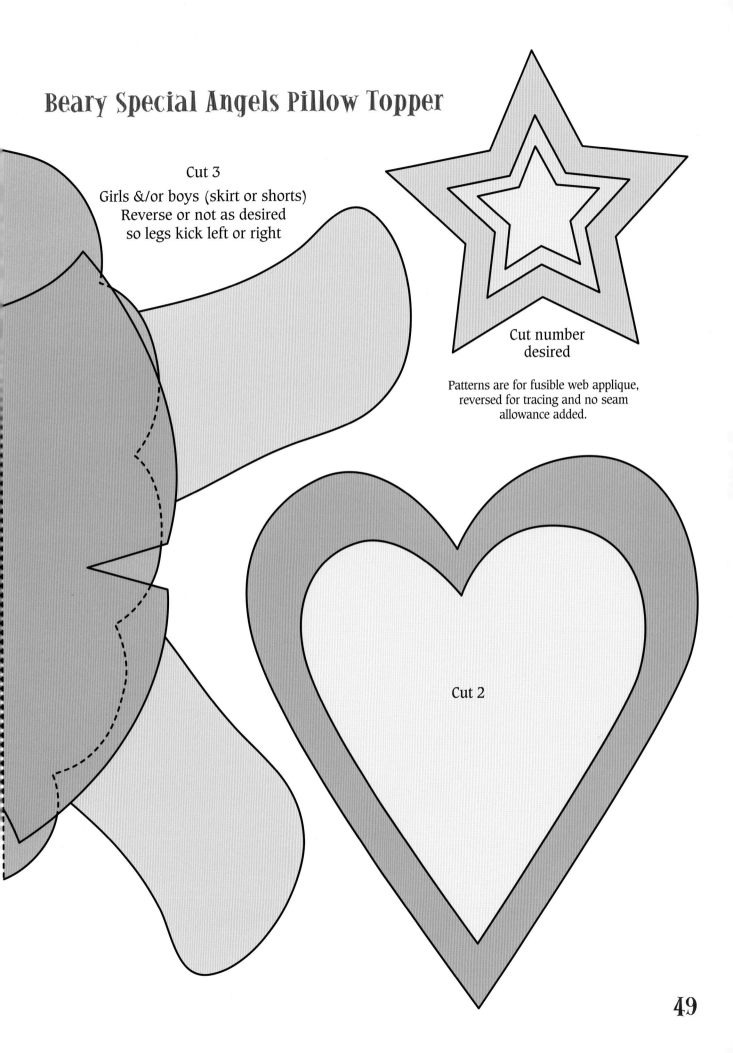

For each flower:
Cut 9

Blue Dahlia Topper

For each flower:
Cut 3

Be Mine Pillow Topper

T - Cut 2, cut 2 reversed
D/Q - Cut 2, cut 3 reversed
K - Cut 3, cut 4 reversed

50

Patterns are for fusible web applique, reversed
for tracing and no seam allowance added.

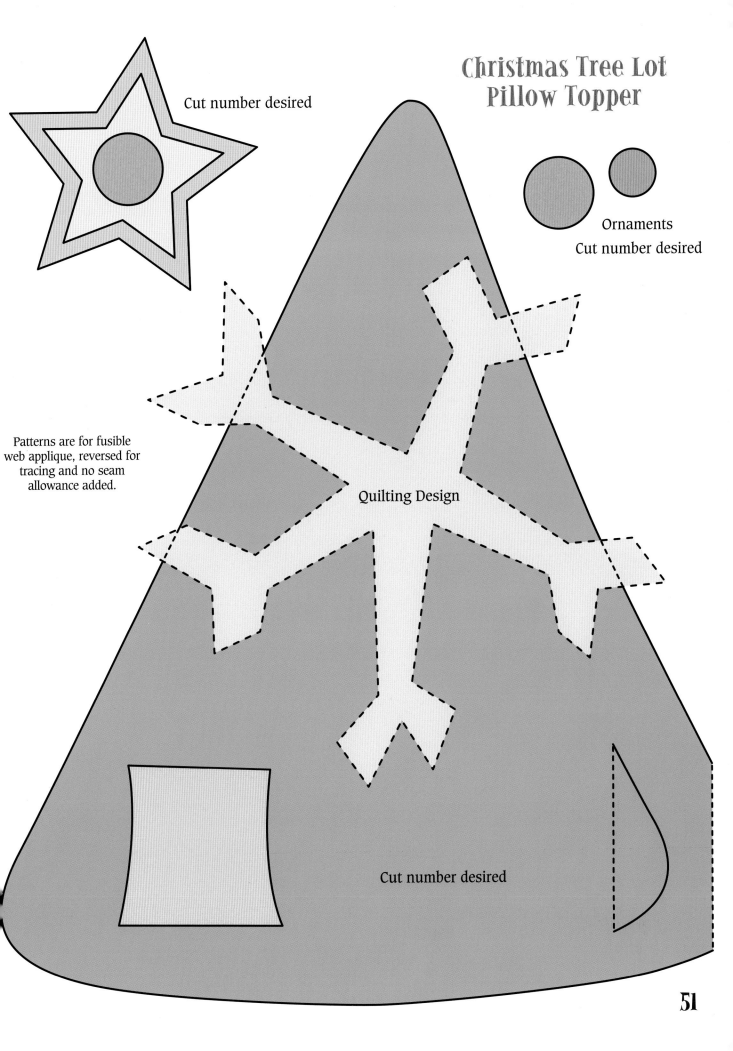

Cut number desired

Ornaments
Cut number desired

Patterns are for fusible
web applique, reversed for
tracing and no seam
allowance added.

Quilting Design

Cut number desired

Christmas Tree Lot Pillow Topper

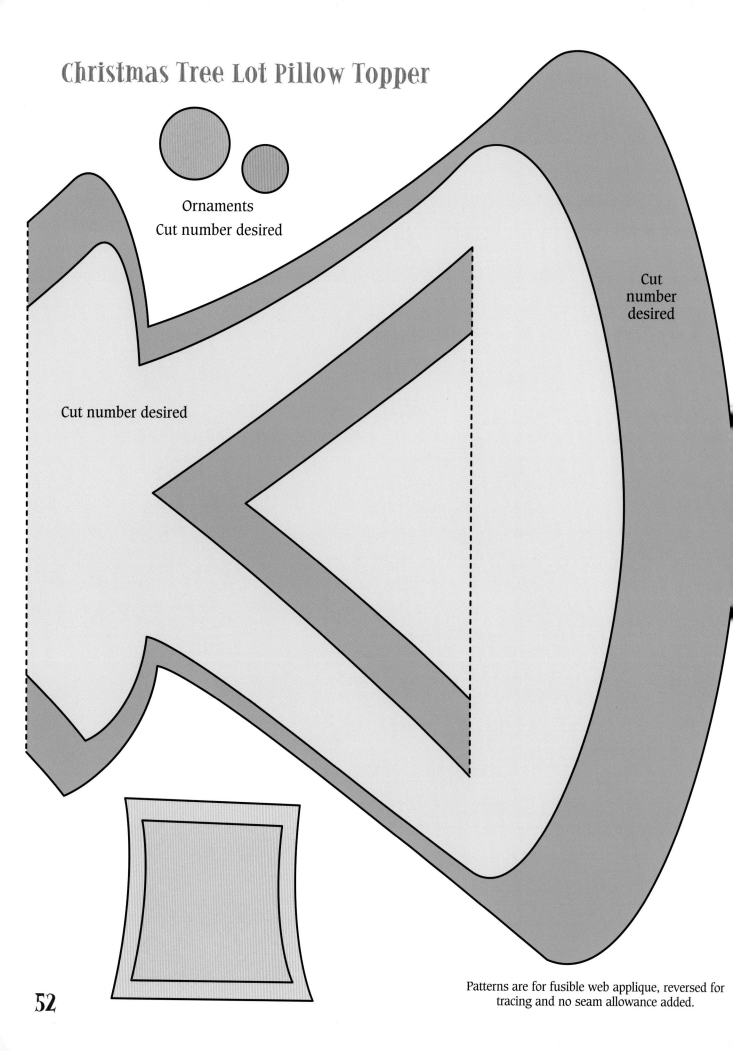

Ornaments
Cut number desired

Cut number desired

Cut
number
desired

Patterns are for fusible web applique, reversed for
tracing and no seam allowance added.

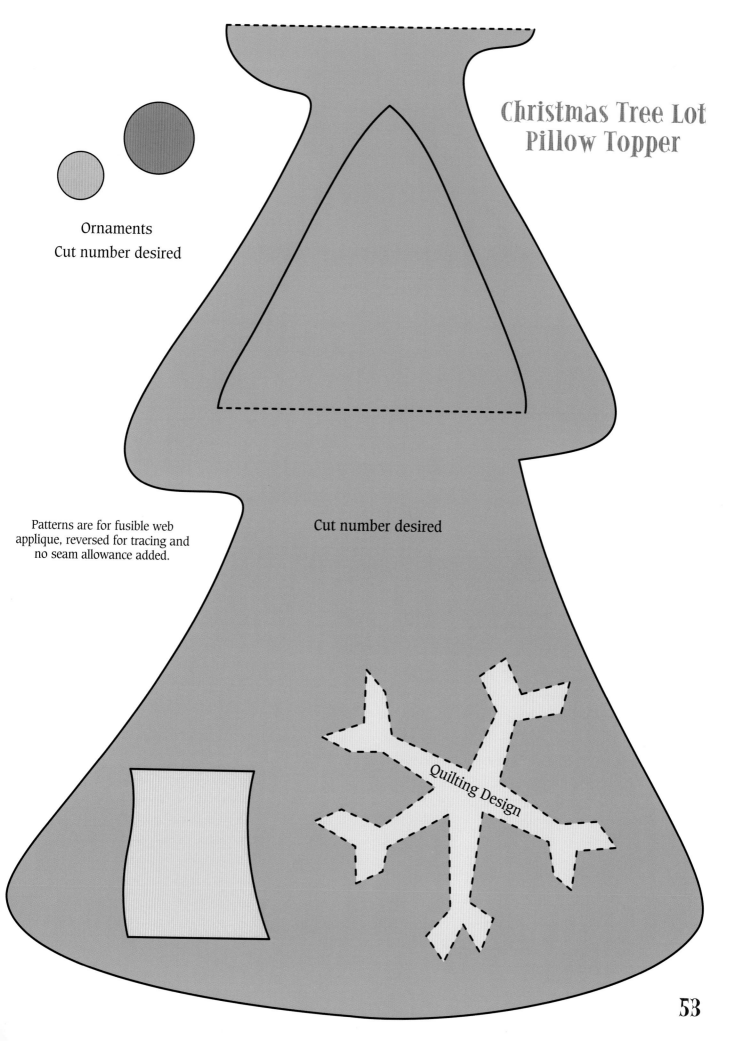

Ornaments
Cut number desired

Patterns are for fusible web applique, reversed for tracing and no seam allowance added.

Cut number desired

Christmas Tree Lot
Pillow Topper

Quilting Design

Apartment Life
Pillow Topper

Patterns are for fusible web applique, reversed
for tracing and no seam allowance added.

Apartment Life Pillow Topper

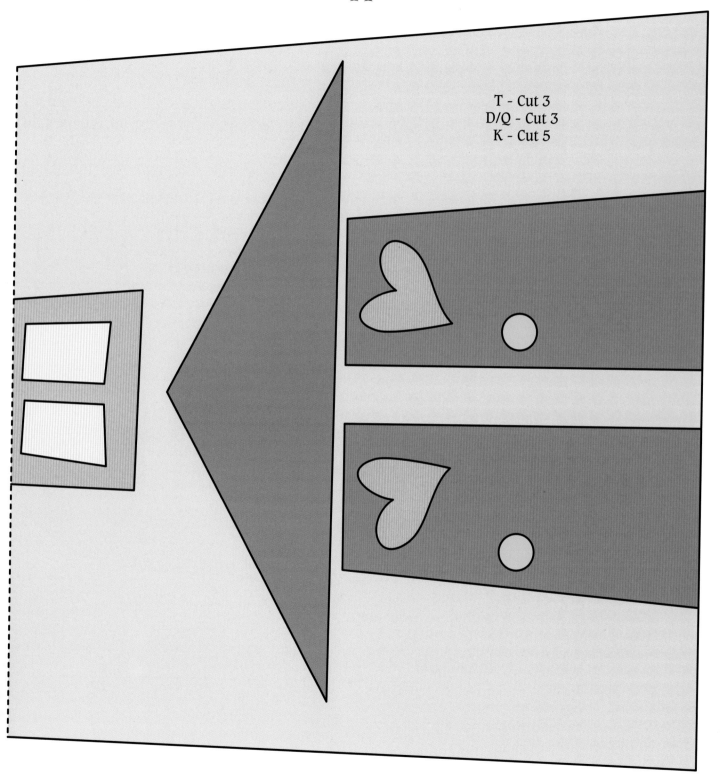

T - Cut 3
D/Q - Cut 3
K - Cut 5

Patterns are for fusible web applique, reversed for tracing and no seam allowance added.

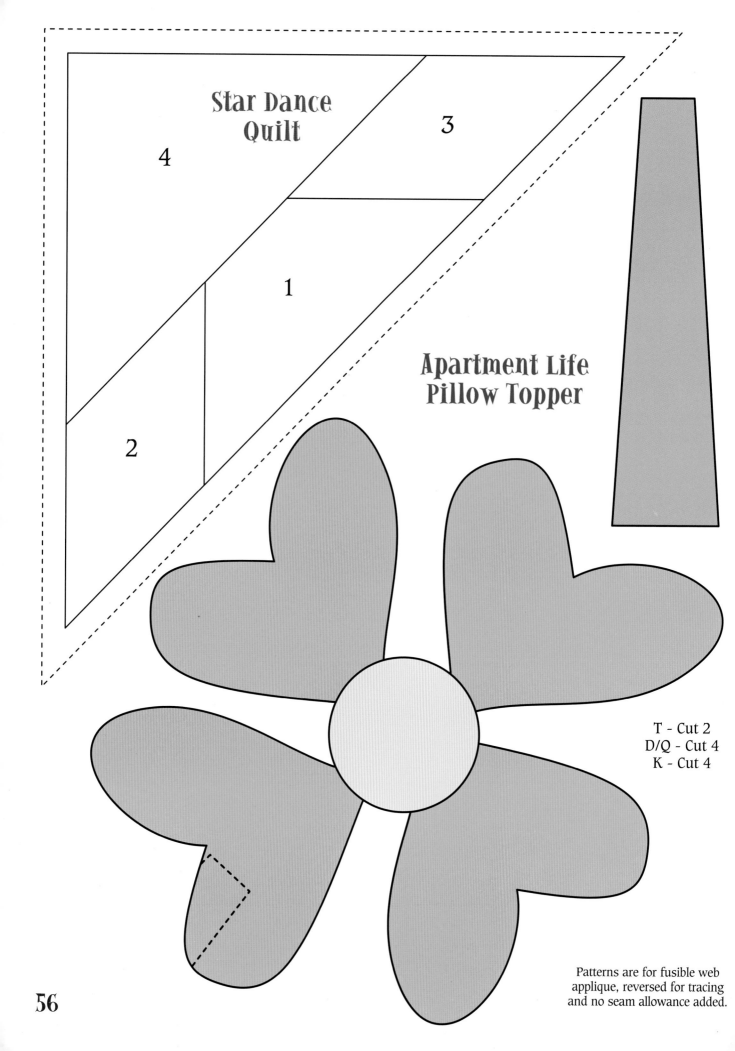

Star Dance Quilt

4

3

1

2

Apartment Life Pillow Topper

T - Cut 2
D/Q - Cut 4
K - Cut 4

Patterns are for fusible web applique, reversed for tracing and no seam allowance added.